BRAND BUILDING FOR BEGINNERS

How To Increase Your Brand's Reach And Make Sales By Using Social Media Platforms

Andrew Taylor

Copyright © 2024 By Andrew Taylor

All rights reserved. No part of this publication may be reproduced, distributed, or transmitted in any form or by any means, including photocopying, recording, or other electronic or mechanical methods, without the prior written permission of the publisher, except in the case of brief quotations embodied in critical reviews and certain other noncommercial uses permitted by copyright law.

Table of Contents

Chapter 1 7
Understanding Social Media Marketing 7
   Key Social Media Platforms and Their Unique Features 7
   Understanding Your Target Audience 10
   Setting Clear and Achievable Goals 16
   Conducting a Social Media Audit 20

Chapter 2 25
Building a Strong Social Media Presence 25
   Creating a Compelling Brand Identity 25
   Creating and Curating Engaging Content 29
   The Art of Storytelling in Social Media 32
   Visual Branding: Graphics, Photos, and Videos 36

Chapter 3 41
Strategies for Increasing Reach 41
   Leveraging Social Media Algorithms: How They Work and How to Use Them 41
   Organic Growth Strategies 44
   Paid Advertising: When and How to Invest 49
   Collaborations and Influencer Marketing 53

Chapter 4 57

Engaging and Retaining Your Audience 57

Building Community: Interaction and Engagement.................. 57

Customer Service Through Social Media 61

Monitoring and Responding to Feedback 64

Creating Loyalty Programs and Incentives 66

Chapter 5 71

Measuring Success and Making Adjustments........................ 71

Key Metrics to Track for social media marketing.................... 71

Tools and Analytics for Social Media...................................... 75

A/B Testing: What It Is and Why It Matters 78

Adapting Strategies in Response to Performance Data............. 84

Chapter 6 87

Advanced Tactics and Future Trends...................................... 87

The Role of AI and Automation in Social Media 87

Exploring Emerging Platforms and Features 91

Staying Ahead: Trends to Watch in Social Media Marketing .. 94

Case Studies of Successful Social Media Campaigns............... 97

Conclusion 105

Introduction

Sarah stared at the analytics dashboard; her brow furrowed in frustration. Despite her best efforts, her small business's social media presence seemed stagnant, with little growth in followers and engagement. "There has to be a better way to get my brand in front of potential customers," she muttered to herself.

As the founder of a handmade jewelry line, Sarah knew she needed to find a solution fast. Competition was fierce, and her online sales were not keeping up with her production. She had poured her heart and soul into building this business, and she wasn't about to let it fall for lack of visibility.

Determined, Sarah began researching strategies to boost her brand's reach on social media. She learned about the power of brand building and influencer marketing, optimizing her content for different platforms, and running targeted ad campaigns. With a renewed sense of purpose, she set out to transform her social media presence from a liability to a major asset for her business.

In the past, Sarah had dabbled in social media, posting photos of her latest creations and hoping that her followers would share them with their friends. But her follower count remained stubbornly low, and her posts were often lost in the endless scroll of her audience's feeds. She knew she needed to take a more strategic approach if she wanted to see real results.

As she delved deeper into the world of social media marketing, Sarah discovered a wealth of tools and tactics that could help her reach a much wider audience. She learned how to craft compelling

content that would capture the attention of her
target customers, and how to use hashtags, geotargeting, and other optimization techniques to ensure that her posts were seen by the right people.

One of the most powerful strategies Sarah discovered was the power of brand building. By partnering with respected figures in her industry, she was able to tap into their established audiences and gain exposure to a whole new pool of potential customers. She carefully vetted potential influencers to ensure that their values and brand image aligned with her own, and crafted collaborative campaigns that provided value to both parties.

In addition to her brand outreach, Sarah also began running targeted social media ad campaigns. By leveraging the rich data and targeting capabilities of platforms like Facebook and Instagram, she was able to reach her ideal customers with laser-like precision. She experimented with different ad formats, messaging, and targeting strategies to optimize her campaigns for maximum return on investment.

The results of Sarah's efforts were nothing short of transformative. Within a matter of months, her Instagram following had grown exponentially, and her online sales had skyrocketed. Customers were raving about her brand, and she was receiving inquiries from wholesale buyers and boutique owners who wanted to carry her products.

As Sarah looked back on her journey, she was filled with a sense of pride and accomplishment. She had taken a risk, stepped out of her comfort zone, and learned how to harness the power of social media to take her business to new heights. And now, she was ready to share her secrets with other entrepreneurs who were looking to do the same.

Chapter 1

Understanding Social Media Marketing

Key Social Media Platforms and Their Unique Features

In the ever-evolving digital landscape, social media platforms have become an integral part of our daily lives, shaping the way we communicate, share information, and connect with others. Each platform offers its unique features, catering to the diverse needs and preferences of users worldwide.

Facebook: The Social Networking Powerhouse

Facebook, launched in 2004, has undoubtedly become the most ubiquitous social media platform, boasting over 2.7 billion monthly active users as of 2023. Its core features include personal profile pages, news feeds, and the ability to connect with friends, family, and communities through sharing posts, photos, and updates. One of Facebook's standout features is its robust event planning and group functionalities, allowing users to organize and attend virtual or in-person events, as well as join and participate in discussions within niche communities.

Instagram: Visual Storytelling at Its Finest

Acquired by Facebook in 2012, Instagram has carved out its niche as a visual-centric social media platform. With its focus on photo and video sharing, Instagram has become a haven for aspiring and professional photographers, influencers, and businesses. The platform's signature features, such as the classic square-format photos, Stories (ephemeral content that disappears after 24 hours), and the ever-popular Instagram Reels (short-form video content), have revolutionized the way users share and consume visual content.

Twitter: The Real-Time Information Hub

Launched in 2006, Twitter has established itself as a fast-paced, real-time information hub, where users can share and consume bite-sized updates, known as "tweets." The platform's unique features, such as the 280-character limit, hashtags, and the ability to "retweet" or "like" content, have made it a go-to platform for breaking news, social activism, and real-time conversations. Twitter's dynamic nature has also made it a powerful platform for businesses and individuals to engage with their audiences and stay up-to-date on the latest trends and discussions.

LinkedIn: The Professional Networking Giant

Designed for professional networking and career development, LinkedIn has become the premier platform for individuals to showcase their skills, experience, and connections. The platform allows users to create detailed personal profiles, connect with colleagues and industry peers, and engage in discussions within specific professional communities. One of LinkedIn's standout features is its robust job search and recruitment functionalities, making it a valuable tool for both job seekers and employers.

TikTok: The Viral Video Sensation

Emerging as a global phenomenon in recent years, TikTok has captured the attention of a younger demographic with its unique short-form video format. The platform's algorithm-driven "For You" feed, which curates content based on user preferences and engagement, has made it a hub for viral trends, challenges, and creative content. TikTok's seamless video editing tools, diverse music library, and the ability to collaborate with other users have contributed to its meteoric rise in popularity, particularly among Gen Z and Millennial audiences.

YouTube: The Video Streaming Giant

YouTube, the world's largest video-sharing platform, has revolutionized the way we consume and create content. Launched in 2005, YouTube offers a vast library of user-generated and professional video content, spanning diverse categories such as entertainment, education, tutorials, and more. The platform's features, including the ability to subscribe to channels, comment on videos, and create playlists, have fostered a vibrant community of content creators and viewers.

Snapchat: The Ephemeral Social Network

Snapchat, introduced in 2011, has carved out a unique niche in the social media landscape with its focus on ephemeral content. The platform's key feature is the "Snap," a photo or video that disappears after being viewed, encouraging spontaneity and in-the-moment sharing. Snapchat also offers innovative features like augmented reality-powered lenses, location-based geofilters, and the ability to create "Stories" that can be viewed by friends for 24 hours.

These social media platforms, each with its distinct features and user experiences, have transformed the way we connect, share, and consume information in the digital age. As technology continues to evolve, the landscape of social media will undoubtedly continue to adapt and expand, presenting new and exciting opportunities for users to explore and engage with the world around them.

Understanding Your Target Audience

Successful businesses and marketing campaigns are built on a deep understanding of the target audience. Who are you trying to reach? What are their needs, desires, pain points, and preferences? Answering these questions is crucial for crafting effective messaging, choosing the right marketing channels, and developing products or services that truly resonate.

The practical strategies for developing a crystal-clear picture of your target audience. From conducting market research to creating detailed buyer personas, you'll gain the insights you need to attract, engage, and convert your ideal customers.

Identifying Your Target Audience

The first step in understanding your audience is clearly defining who they are. This goes far beyond simple demographics like age, gender, and location. To truly connect with your target market, you need to dig deeper and uncover there:

- **Psychographics:** What are their values, interests, attitudes, and lifestyles?

- **Behaviors:** How do they research and make purchasing decisions? What media do they consume?

- **Challenges and pain points:** What problems are they struggling to solve? What barriers are they facing?
- **Aspirations:** What are their goals and dreams? What motivates them to take action?

One of the best ways to gather this information is through market research. This may involve:

- Surveys and questionnaires
- Focus groups and interviews
- Social media listening
- Competitor analysis
- Industry reports and data

As you collect this data, look for patterns and trends that can help you paint a vivid picture of your ideal customer. This will form the foundation for your buyer personas.

Developing Buyer Personas

Buyer personas are semi-fictional representations of your target customers. These detailed profiles go beyond surface-level demographics to capture the motivations, behaviors, and pain points that drive your audience's decision-making.

Effective buyer personas typically include information such as:

- Personal background (age, location, family status, etc.)
- Job title, industry, and responsibilities
- Values, interests, and lifestyle
- Typical day-to-day activities
- Primary goals and challenges

- Buying behaviors and decision-making process
- Preferred communication channels

The more specific and detailed your personas are, the better you'll be able to tailor your marketing and product development to their unique needs. Consider creating 3-5 personas that represent your core target segments.

To develop these personas, you can draw from the market research you conducted earlier, as well as:

- Interviews with existing customer

- Conversations with your sales and customer service teams

- Industry benchmarks and data

As you flesh out each persona, keep the following principles in mind:

- **Make them realistic:** Personas should be based on real data, not just guesswork.

- **Focus on their needs:** Understand what motivates and frustrates your target customers.

- **Differentiate between segments:** Each persona should have distinct attributes that set them apart.
- **Prioritize your personas:** Identify your most valuable or high-potential customer segments.

With robust buyer personas in hand, you'll be able to tailor your messaging, channels, and overall marketing strategy to speak directly to the needs and preferences of your target audience.

Ongoing Audience Research and Refinement

Your target audience is not static - it evolves as customer behaviors, preferences, and market conditions change. That's why it's crucial to approach audience research as an ongoing process, not a one-time exercise.

Regularly review and update your buyer personas to ensure they remain accurate and relevant. This may involve:

- Conducting additional surveys, interviews, and focus groups
- Analyzing website analytics, social media engagement, and sales data
- Monitoring industry trends and competitive shifts

As you gather new insights, look for opportunities to refine your personas or even create new ones to address emerging customer segments.

It's also important to involve cross-functional teams in this process. Sales, customer service, and product development teams often have valuable firsthand knowledge of your target audience that can supplement your research findings.

By maintaining a dynamic, data-driven understanding of your customers, you'll be able to adapt your marketing strategies and offerings to capitalize on changing needs and preferences. This agility is key to staying ahead of the competition and driving long-term business growth.

Activating Your Audience Insights

Once you've developed a deep understanding of your target audience, the real work begins - putting those insights into action. Here are some ways to leverage your buyer personas to enhance your marketing and product development efforts:

Personalized Messaging and Content: Use the detailed profile information in your personas to craft hyper-targeted messaging, content, and creative assets that speak directly to your audience's pain points, interests, and preferences.

Optimized Channel Selection: Determine which marketing channels (social media, email, paid advertising, etc.) are most effective for reaching and engaging your target customers based on their media consumption habits and buying behaviors.

Tailored Product Development: Align your product roadmap and feature sets with the specific needs and pain points identified in your buyer personas. This ensures you're delivering solutions that truly resonate with your audience.

Enhanced Customer Experience: Apply persona insights to optimize the customer journey, from the initial touchpoints to post-purchase support. This can involve everything from website UX to sales enablement tools to customer service protocols.

Hyper-Targeted Advertising: Use persona data to inform highly segmented advertising campaigns that serve the right message to the right audience at the right time, maximizing relevance and impact.

Data-Driven Decision Making: Leverage persona insights to inform strategic business decisions across marketing, sales, product, and other key functions. This can help you allocate resources more effectively and capitalize on emerging opportunities.

By weaving your audience's understanding throughout your organization, you'll create a powerful feedback loop that drives continuous improvement and growth. Stay attuned to your customers' evolving needs, and you'll be poised to deliver exceptional value and keep them engaged for the long haul.

Understanding your target audience is the foundation for building a successful, customer-centric business. By conducting thorough market research, developing robust buyer personas, and activating those insights across your organization, you'll be equipped to attract, engage, and delight your ideal customers.

Audience research is an ongoing process, not a one-time exercise. Stay curious, adaptable, and responsive to the changing needs of your market. With a deep, data-driven understanding of your target audience, you'll be able to outmaneuver the competition and achieve sustainable growth.

Setting Clear and Achievable Goals

Achieving our goals is one of the most rewarding and fulfilling experiences in life. It gives us a sense of purpose, boosts our confidence, and helps us grow as individuals. However, the path to achieving our goals is not always straightforward. It's easy to become overwhelmed by the sheer magnitude of our aspirations, leading us to either abandon them altogether or struggle to make any meaningful progress.

The secret to overcoming these challenges lies in setting clear and achievable goals. By breaking down our big dreams into smaller, more manageable steps, we can create a roadmap that makes the journey feel less daunting and more attainable.

Understand Your WHY

Before we can set our goals, it's essential to understand our underlying motivation – our "why." Why do we want to achieve this particular goal? What impact will it have on our lives or the lives of others? Connecting with our deeper purpose will not only help us stay motivated, but it will also guide us in making decisions and staying on track.

For example, if your goal is to start a business, your "why" might be to create financial independence and have more control over your time. Or if your goal is to get in shape, your "why" might be to improve your health and energy levels so you can enjoy your favorite activities without limitations.

Define SMART Goals

Once we've identified our "why," the next step is to define our goals using the SMART framework: Specific, Measurable, Achievable, Relevant, and Time-bound.

Specific: Instead of setting a vague goal like "lose weight," be as specific as possible. For example, "Lose 10 pounds by June 30th."

Measurable: Quantify your goal so you can track your progress. In the weight loss example, the "10 pounds" makes the goal measurable.

Achievable: Set goals that stretch you, but are still within the realm of possibility. While it's great to dream big, setting unrealistic goals can lead to disappointment and discouragement.

Relevant: Ensure your goals align with your values and overall life plan. This will help you stay motivated and focused.

Time-bound: Assign a deadline to your goal, which will create a sense of urgency and help you stay accountable.

By defining your goals using the SMART framework, you'll create a clear roadmap that will guide you toward success.

Break It Down

Once you have your SMART goals in place, the next step is to break them down into smaller, more manageable action steps. This will help you stay focused and motivated, as crossing off each completed task will give you a sense of progress and accomplishment.

For example, if your goal is to start a business, your action steps might include:

1. Research and identify a viable business idea
2. Develop a business plan
3. Secure financing
4. Register the business
5. Set up your website and online presence
6. Acquire necessary licenses and permits
7. Hire your first employee

By breaking down your goal into these smaller, actionable steps, you can tackle it one piece at a time, rather than feeling overwhelmed by the entire project.

Celebrate Milestones

As you work towards your goals, it's important to celebrate your milestones along the way. This will help you stay motivated and reinforce the progress you're making.

Whether it's hitting a weight loss target, securing your first client, or reaching a sales goal, take the time to acknowledge and appreciate your achievements. This could be as simple as treating yourself to a special meal, or as elaborate as planning a celebratory event with friends and family.

Celebrating your milestones not only boosts your morale but also helps you stay focused and committed to your long-term objectives.

Adjust and Adapt

It's important to remember that goal setting is not a one-time event, but an ongoing process. As you work towards your goals, you may encounter unexpected challenges or discover that your initial plan needs to be adjusted.

Be willing to adapt and make changes as needed. This might mean revising your timeline, modifying your action steps, or even reevaluating your ultimate goal. The key is to remain flexible and open to new possibilities, rather than stubbornly sticking to a plan that is no longer serving you.

By embracing a growth mindset and being willing to adjust your approach, you'll be better equipped to navigate the ups and downs of the goal-achieving journey.

Setting clear and achievable goals is the cornerstone of personal and professional success. By understanding our "why," defining SMART goals, breaking them down into actionable steps, celebrating our milestones, and being willing to adapt, we can transform our dreams into reality.

The path to achieving our goals may not always be linear, but with persistence, dedication, and a willingness to learn and grow, we can overcome any obstacle that stands in our way. So, let's embrace the challenge and embark on a journey of self-discovery and fulfillment.

Conducting a Social Media Audit

In the ever-evolving digital landscape, social media has become an integral part of our personal and professional lives. It's a powerful tool that can help businesses and individuals alike to connect, engage, and build meaningful relationships with their target audience. However, to truly harness the full potential of social media, it's crucial to conduct a comprehensive social media audit. This process allows you to assess the effectiveness of your current social media strategies, identify areas for improvement, and develop a plan to optimize your online presence.

Understanding the Importance of a Social Media Audit

A social media audit is more than just a routine check-up; it's a transformative process that can propel your digital marketing efforts to new heights. By conducting a thorough audit, you gain invaluable insights into your audience's behavior, the performance of your content, and the overall health of your social media channels. This knowledge empowers you to make informed decisions, refine your strategies, and ultimately, achieve your desired goals.

Step 1: Defining Your Objectives

Before diving into the audit process, it's essential to clearly define your objectives. What do you hope to achieve through your social media presence? Are you aiming to increase brand awareness, drive traffic to your website, generate leads, or enhance customer engagement? By setting specific, measurable, achievable, relevant, and time-bound (SMART) goals, you can ensure that your audit is focused and tailored to your unique needs.

Step 2: Inventory Your Social Media Channels

The next step is to take a comprehensive inventory of all your social media channels, including the platforms you're actively using, as well as any dormant or abandoned accounts. This will give you a complete picture of your online presence and help you identify opportunities for consolidation or expansion.

For each channel, gather the following information:

- Username or handle
- Date of creation
- Number of followers or connections
- Engagement metrics (likes, comments, shares)
- Content types and frequency of posting
- Branding elements (profile image, cover photo, bio, etc.)

Step 3: Analyze Your Audience and Engagement

One of the most valuable insights you can gain from a social media audit is a deep understanding of your audience. Dive into the demographics, interests, and behaviors of your followers across each platform. Look for patterns and trends that can inform your content strategy and help you better tailor your messaging to your target audience.

Additionally, evaluate your engagement metrics, such as likes, comments, shares, and click-through rates. This will help you identify which types of content resonate most with your audience and where you may need to adjust your approach.

Step 4: Assess Content Performance

Closely examine the performance of your social media content, including the types of posts, the frequency of publishing, and the overall engagement they generate. Look for patterns and trends that may indicate which content is most effective in driving your desired outcomes.

Consider factors such as:

- ➢ Post format (text, image, video, poll, etc.)
- ➢ Posting times and days
- ➢ Captions and copy
- ➢ Use of hashtags, mentions and calls to action

By analyzing this data, you can refine your content strategy and focus on the types of posts that consistently perform well.

Step 5: Evaluate Your Competitors

Keeping an eye on your competition is essential in the social media landscape. Conduct a competitive analysis to understand how your peers and industry leaders are leveraging social media to connect with their audience. This can provide valuable insights into best practices, emerging trends, and potential areas of opportunity for your social media strategy.

Step 6: Identify Strengths, Weaknesses, Opportunities, and Threats (SWOT)

With all the data gathered from the previous steps, it's time to synthesize the information and conduct a SWOT
analysis. This will help you identify your social media strengths, weaknesses, opportunities, and threats, allowing you to make

informed decisions about where to focus your efforts and resources.

Step 7: Develop a Strategic Action Plan

Armed with the insights gleaned from your social media audit, you can now develop a strategic action plan to optimize your online presence. This plan should include specific, actionable steps to address the areas identified in your SWOT analysis, such as:

- Updating your social media profiles and branding
- Refining your content strategy and posting schedule
- Exploring new platforms or channels to expand your reach
- Enhancing engagement through targeted campaigns or influencer partnerships
- Implementing tools and analytics to monitor and measure your performance

Conducting a comprehensive social media audit is a transformative process that can propel your digital marketing efforts to new heights. By understanding your audience, evaluating your content performance, and identifying areas for improvement, you can develop a strategic action plan to optimize your online presence and achieve your desired goals.

The social media landscape is ever-evolving, so it's essential to make this audit a regular part of your digital marketing strategy. Embrace the insights you gain and be prepared to adapt and evolve your approach as new trends and best practices emerge.

Embark on this journey of social media optimization and unlock the full potential of your online presence. The rewards will be well worth the effort.

Chapter 2

Building a Strong Social Media Presence

Creating a Compelling Brand Identity

In the dynamic landscape of modern business, a strong and compelling brand identity has become a vital asset for any organization seeking to thrive and succeed. Your brand identity is the foundation upon which you build lasting connections with your target audience, differentiate yourself from the competition, and ultimately, drive the growth and success of your enterprise.

The Importance of a Compelling Brand Identity

A compelling brand identity is more than just a logo or a catchy slogan. It is a carefully crafted representation of your company's values, personality, and unique offering. It is the first impression that potential customers and clients will have of your business, and it can make all the difference in whether they choose to engage with your products or services.

A strong brand identity helps to:

1. **Stand Out in a Crowded Marketplace**: In today's hyper-competitive business environment, standing out from the crowd is essential. A compelling brand identity allows you

to cut through the noise and capture the attention of your target audience.

2. **Build Trust and Credibility**: A well-designed and consistent brand identity conveys professionalism, reliability, and trustworthiness, which are all crucial factors in establishing long-lasting relationships with your customers.

3. **Foster Emotional Connections**: The most successful brands are those that can evoke an emotional response from their audience. A compelling brand identity can help you create a sense of belonging and loyalty among your customers.

4. **Increase Brand Recognition**: A strong and recognizable brand identity can help your business become more memorable and top-of-mind with your target audience, leading to increased brand awareness and potentially higher sales.

Elements of a Compelling Brand Identity

Crafting a compelling brand identity requires a thoughtful and strategic approach, encompassing several key elements:

1. **Logo**: Your logo is the visual representation of your brand and should be designed to be memorable, distinctive, and reflective of your brand's personality and values.

2. **Color Palette**: The colors you choose for your brand identity should be carefully selected to convey the right emotions and align with your brand's personality.

3. **Typography**: The fonts and typefaces you use should be both visually appealing and easy to read, reinforcing the overall tone and style of your brand.

4. **Brand Messaging**: Your brand messaging, including your tagline, value proposition, and key messaging points, should be crafted to resonate with your target audience and effectively communicate what sets your brand apart.

5. **Brand Imagery**: The visual elements of your brand, such as photography, illustrations, and graphics, should work together to create a cohesive and visually appealing brand aesthetic.

6. **Brand Tone and Voice**: The way you communicate with your audience, both in written and verbal form, should be consistent with your brand's personality and values.

Developing a Compelling Brand Identity

Developing a compelling brand identity is a multi-step process that requires careful planning, research, and execution. Here are the key steps:

1. **Define Your Brand's Purpose and Values**: Start by clearly defining your brand's purpose, mission, and core

values. This will provide the foundation for your brand identity and guide all of your branding decisions.

2. **Conduct Market Research**: Understand your target audience, their needs, and their perceptions of your brand and competitors. This will help you create a brand identity that resonates with your ideal customers.

3. **Develop Your Brand Positioning**: Determine how you want your brand to be perceived by your target audience and how it differs from the competition. This will inform the development of your brand messaging and visual identity.

4. **Create a Cohesive Visual Identity**: Develop a consistent and visually appealing brand identity that includes your logo, color palette, typography, and other visual elements. Ensure that these elements work together to create a cohesive and memorable brand aesthetic.

5. **Establish Brand Guidelines**: Develop a set of brand guidelines that outline how your brand identity should be used across all touchpoints, including your website, marketing materials, and social media channels.

6. **Consistently Implement Your Brand Identity**: Ensure that your brand identity is consistently implemented across all aspects of your business, from your customer-facing communications to your internal operations. This will help to reinforce your brand's credibility and authenticity.

Creating a compelling brand identity is a critical step in the success of any business. By carefully crafting a brand that resonates with your target audience, you can differentiate yourself from the competition, build trust and loyalty, and ultimately, drive the growth and success of your organization. By following the steps outlined in this article, you can develop a powerful and engaging brand identity that will help your business thrive in today's dynamic market.

Creating and Curating Engaging Content

In today's content-saturated digital landscape, capturing the attention of your audience has never been more crucial. Whether you're running a blog, managing a corporate website, or crafting social media posts, the ability to create and curate engaging content is the key to standing out from the crowd and building a loyal following.

Engaging content doesn't just happen by chance; it requires a strategic approach that takes into account the preferences, pain points, and desires of your target audience. By understanding what resonates with your readers, you can craft content that not only informs and educates but also inspires, entertains, and compels them to take action.

Identifying Your Audience and Their Needs

The first step in creating engaging content is to have a deep understanding of your target audience. Who are they? What are their interests, challenges, and aspirations? What type of content are they most likely to consume and share?

Conduct thorough audience research, analyze your existing data, and create detailed buyer personas to get a clear picture of who you're speaking to. This information will guide your content creation process and ensure that your efforts are aligned with the needs and preferences of your audience.

Crafting Captivating Content

With a solid understanding of your audience, you can begin crafting content that captures their attention and resonates with them on a deeper level. Here are some key strategies to consider:

Storytelling

Humans are hardwired to respond to stories. By weaving narratives into your content, you can create an emotional connection with your audience and make your message more memorable. Incorporate real-life examples, personal anecdotes, and relatable characters to bring your content to life.

Visuals

The human brain processes visual information 60,000 times faster than text. Leverage the power of images, infographics, videos, and other multimedia elements to complement your written content and make it more engaging and visually appealing.

Relatable and Authentic Voice

Develop a distinct brand voice that feels genuine, approachable, and aligned with your audience's preferences. Avoid corporate jargon and instead, adopt a conversational tone that makes your readers feel like they're engaging with a trusted friend or subject matter expert.

Interactivity

Encourage your audience to actively participate in your content by incorporating interactive elements such as polls, quizzes, surveys, or even user-generated content. This not only makes your content more engaging but also provides valuable insights that can inform your future content strategies.

Relevance and Timeliness

Stay up-to-date with the latest trends, news, and conversations within your industry or niche. Craft content that addresses your audience's most pressing concerns and aligns with their current interests and pain points.

Curating and Repurposing Content

Creating high-quality, original content can be time-consuming and resource-intensive. To maximize your content's reach and impact, consider curating and repurposing existing content in innovative ways.

Content Curation

Identify and share high-quality, relevant content from industry influencers, thought leaders, and trusted sources. This not only saves you time and effort but also demonstrates your expertise and position as a valuable resource for your audience.

Content Repurposing

Breathe new life into your existing content by repurposing it into different formats, such as blog posts, social media updates, videos, or podcasts. This allows you to extend the lifespan of your content and reach a wider audience through multiple channels.

Measuring and Optimizing Your Content

Regularly analyze the performance of your content to identify what's working and what needs improvement. Utilize analytics tools, track key metrics (such as engagement rates, bounce rates, and conversion rates), and gather feedback from your audience to continuously refine and optimize your content strategy.

By following these strategies, you can create and curate engaging content that captivates your audience, establishes your expertise, and drives meaningful results for your business or personal brand.

The Art of Storytelling in Social Media

Storytelling has been a fundamental aspect of human communication since the dawn of civilization. It is the art of weaving words, emotions, and experiences into a captivating narrative that resonates with our audience. In the digital age, where social media has become the dominant platform for sharing and consuming content, the art of storytelling has evolved to become a powerful tool for connecting with others, building brand loyalty, and driving engagement.

Crafting a Compelling Narrative

The foundation of effective storytelling on social media lies in the ability to craft a compelling narrative. This involves more than simply recounting a series of events; it requires the careful selection of details, the development of relatable characters, and the incorporation of emotional elements that draw the audience in.

One of the key elements of a successful social media story is the use of a consistent, authentic voice. This means that the narrative should reflect the brand's personality, values, and tone of communication. By maintaining a consistent voice, businesses can create a strong, recognizable brand identity that helps to build trust and loyalty with their audience.

Another important aspect of crafting a compelling narrative is the use of visual elements. In the age of Instagram and TikTok, visuals have become an integral part of social media storytelling. Whether it's high-quality photographs, eye-catching graphics, or engaging video content, the effective use of visuals can help bring the story to life and make it more memorable for the audience.

Leveraging Emotional Connections

Effective storytelling on social media is not just about relaying information; it's about creating an emotional connection with the audience. By tapping into the emotions of their followers, businesses can cultivate a deeper sense of engagement and loyalty.

One way to achieve this is through the use of personal narratives. By sharing stories that are rooted in the experiences and perspectives of the brand or its representatives, businesses can create a sense of authenticity and vulnerability that resonates with their audience. This can be particularly powerful in industries where personal connections and trust are crucial, such as healthcare, wellness, or personal finance.

Another way to leverage emotional connections is through the use of storytelling techniques that evoke specific emotions, such as humor, inspiration, or nostalgia. By carefully crafting narratives that tap into these emotional triggers, businesses can create content that is not only engaging but also memorable and shareable.

Fostering Audience Engagement

Effective social media storytelling is not a one-way street; it requires a deep understanding of the audience and a willingness to engage with them in meaningful ways. This means listening to their feedback, responding to their questions and comments, and actively incorporating their perspectives into the ongoing narrative.

One way to foster audience engagement is through the use of interactive elements, such as polls, quizzes, or ask-me-anything sessions. By inviting the audience to participate in the storytelling process, businesses can create a sense of community and ownership that can lead to increased loyalty and advocacy.

Another way to foster audience engagement is through the use of user-generated content. By encouraging followers to share their own stories, experiences, and perspectives, businesses can not only deepen their connection with the audience but also generate a steady stream of authentic, shareable content.

Adapting to Changing Trends and Platforms

The social media landscape is constantly evolving, with new platforms, features, and trends emerging all the time. To remain effective, businesses must be willing to adapt their storytelling strategies to keep pace with these changes.

This may involve experimenting with new formats, such as short-form video content on TikTok or ephemeral stories on Instagram, or exploring emerging technologies, such as augmented reality or interactive virtual experiences. By staying agile and responsive to the changing needs and preferences of their audience, businesses can ensure that their storytelling efforts remain relevant and engaging.

In the ever-changing world of social media, the art of storytelling has become an essential tool for businesses seeking to connect with their audience, build brand loyalty, and drive engagement. By crafting compelling narratives, leveraging emotional connections, fostering audience engagement, and adapting to changing trends and platforms, businesses can harness the power of social media storytelling to achieve their marketing and communication goals.

Visual Branding: Graphics, Photos, and Videos

In the dynamic world of modern marketing, the power of visual branding cannot be overstated. From the captivating graphics that adorn your website to the emotive photographs that grace your social media pages, every visual element plays a crucial role in shaping the perception of your brand.

The essential aspects of visual branding, exploring the strategic use of graphics, photos, and videos to elevate your brand and connect with your audience.

The Importance of Visual Branding

In today's visually saturated landscape, where attention spans are fleeting, the ability to captivate your audience through compelling visuals has become paramount. Studies have shown that the human brain processes visual information 60,000 times faster than text, making it the primary conduit for brand recognition and recall. Effective visual branding not only enhances your brand's aesthetic appeal but also conveys your brand's personality, values, and unique selling proposition.

Graphics: The Cornerstone of Visual Branding

Graphics are the building blocks of your visual identity, serving as the visual representation of your brand. From your logo and color palette to the iconography and illustrations that accompany your content, each graphic element must be carefully crafted to align with your brand's essence. Consistency is key – by maintaining a cohesive visual language across all touchpoints, you'll strengthen brand recognition and foster a sense of familiarity with your audience.

When designing your graphics, consider the following principles:

1. **Simplicity**: opt for clean, minimalist designs that are easy to comprehend and memorable.

2. **Versatility**: Ensure that your graphics can be seamlessly adapted across various mediums, from digital platforms to print materials.

3. **Emotional Connection**: Strive to evoke emotions and create a visceral response from your audience through your visual aesthetic.

4. **Brand Alignment**: Ensure that every graphic element resonates with your brand's personality, values, and messaging.

Photography: Capturing the Heart of Your Brand

Photographs possess the power to elicit emotions, convey messages, and humanize your brand. Whether it's showcasing your products, highlighting your team, or capturing the essence of your brand's culture, high-quality photography can be a powerful tool in your visual branding arsenal.

When selecting or commissioning photographs, consider the following:

1. **Authenticity**: opt for images that authentically represent your brand and its values, rather than stock photography.

2. **Consistency**: Maintain a cohesive photographic style that aligns with your brand's visual identity.

3. **Storytelling**: Use photographs to tell a compelling narrative about your brand, its products, or its mission.

4. **Emotion**: Strive to evoke emotions, whether it's inspiration, happiness, or a sense of aspirational lifestyle.

Video: The Cinematic Approach to Branding

In an era where video content dominates, incorporating captivating videos into your visual branding strategy can be a powerful differentiator. From product demonstrations and behind-the-scenes glimpses to brand explainer videos and emotive storytelling, video content has the unique ability to engage your audience, convey complex information, and foster a deeper connection with your brand.

When crafting your video content, consider the following:

1. **Narrative**: Develop a compelling narrative that resonates with your target audience and aligns with your brand's messaging.

2. **Production Value**: Invest in high-quality production to ensure that your videos are visually striking and professionally executed.

3. **Optimization**: Tailor your video content for various platforms, ensuring that it is optimized for mobile and social media consumption.

4. **Measurable Impact**: Analyze the performance of your video content to gauge its effectiveness and make data-driven decisions for future campaigns.

Integrating Visual Branding Across Touchpoints

Effective visual branding is not limited to a single platform or medium – it must be seamlessly integrated across all touchpoints, from your website and social media channels to your physical marketing collateral and product packaging. By maintaining a cohesive visual identity, you'll create a consistent brand experience that fosters trust, recognition, and loyalty among your audience.

The journey of visual branding is an ongoing process, one that requires continuous refinement and adaptation to keep pace with evolving trends and the changing needs of your audience. By embracing the power of graphics, photography, and video, you'll elevate your brand, captivate your audience, and establish a lasting, meaningful connection that sets you apart in the competitive marketplace.

Chapter 3

Strategies for Increasing Reach

Leveraging Social Media Algorithms: How They Work and How to Use Them

In the ever-evolving landscape of digital marketing, the power of social media platforms has become undeniable. At the heart of this digital revolution lie the intricate algorithms that drive the visibility and reach of content on these platforms. As businesses and individuals strive to effectively leverage social media to connect with their audience, understanding the inner workings of these algorithms has become a crucial skill.

Understanding Social Media Algorithms

Social media algorithms are complex sets of rules and calculations that determine the prioritization and display of content on a user's feed. These algorithms are designed to provide the most relevant and engaging content to each user, based on a variety of factors.

The Factors That Influence Social Media Algorithms

1. **User Engagement**: Social media platforms closely monitor user interactions, such as likes, comments, shares, and time spent on content. Content that generates high levels of engagement is more likely to be favored by the algorithms.

2. **Timeliness**: Algorithms often prioritize recent and timely content, ensuring that users are presented with the most up-to-date information.

3. **Personal Preferences**: Algorithms learn from a user's past behavior and interactions, tailoring the content display to their individual preferences and interests.

4. **Relationships**: Connections and interactions between users, such as friends, followers, and the accounts they engage with, can influence the visibility of content.

5. **Content Quality**: Platforms strive to promote high-quality, informative, and visually appealing content that provides value to users.

The Evolving Nature of Social Media Algorithms

Social media algorithms are constantly evolving to improve user experience and adapt to changing trends and technologies. Platform owners continuously refine their algorithms to stay ahead of the curve and provide the most relevant and engaging content to their users.

Leveraging Social Media Algorithms

Understanding the underlying mechanics of social media algorithms is essential for effectively leveraging them to your advantage. By adopting strategic approaches, businesses and individuals can optimize their social media presence and increase their reach and engagement.

Producing High-Quality, Engaging Content

The foundation of a successful social media strategy lies in creating content that resonates with your target audience. Focus on producing content that is informative, entertaining, and visually appealing. Utilize relevant keywords, hashtags, and multimedia elements to increase the discoverability of your content.

Timing and Frequency of Posting

Social media algorithms prioritize timely and consistent content. Experiment with different posting schedules and times to determine the optimal frequency and timing for your audience. Monitor your analytics to identify the best days and times to share your content.

Encouraging Engagement

Algorithms favor content that generates high engagement, such as likes, comments, and shares. Encourage your followers to interact with your content by asking thought-provoking questions, running polls, and responding to comments in a timely and meaningful manner.

Leveraging Influencer Partnerships

Collaborating with relevant influencers can be a powerful way to amplify your reach and tap into new audiences. Influencers with established credibility and engaged followings can help boost the visibility and credibility of your content.

Paid Advertising and Boosting

While organic reach is essential, leveraging paid advertising and content boosting can further enhance your social media presence. Utilize the targeting and optimization features offered by social media platforms to ensure your paid content reaches the right audience.

Continuous Monitoring and Adaptation

Regularly analyze your social media performance and adjust your strategies accordingly. Monitor metrics such as reach, engagement, and conversions to identify what content resonates best with your audience. Continuously refine your approach to stay ahead of the evolving social media landscape.

In the dynamic world of social media, understanding, and leveraging algorithms is crucial for businesses and individuals seeking to amplify their online presence and connect with their target audience. By mastering the art of creating high-quality, engaging content and implementing strategic techniques, you can unlock the full potential of social media platforms and thrive in the digital landscape.

Organic Growth Strategies

In the dynamic and ever-evolving world of business, the pursuit of growth is a constant challenge. While some organizations opt for aggressive, capital-intensive expansion strategies, a growing number of savvy entrepreneurs and established companies are turning to a more organic approach. Organic growth strategies, rooted in the careful cultivation of internal resources and market opportunities, offer a sustainable path to long-term success.

Harnessing Internal Strengths

The foundation of organic growth lies in a deep understanding and optimization of a business's core competencies. By focusing on the unique strengths and capabilities that set the company apart, leaders can identify expansion opportunities that align with their existing expertise.

Leveraging Existing Capabilities

One of the key tenets of organic growth is the strategic leveraging of a company's existing capabilities. This might involve expanding product lines or service offerings that seamlessly complement the organization's core offerings, allowing for a natural extension of the brand and a deeper connection with the target audience.

Take, for example, a successful specialty coffee roaster who decides to open a chain of cafes. By capitalizing on its expertise in sourcing and roasting high-quality beans, the company can create a distinctive dining experience that resonates with its dedicated customer base, while also generating additional revenue streams.

Fostering Innovation

Organic growth also thrives on a culture of innovation, where employees are encouraged to explore new ideas and experiment with novel approaches. By investing in research and development, businesses can uncover innovative products, services, or processes that can be scaled up and integrated into existing operations.

Consider the case of a software company that decides to develop a cutting-edge data analytics platform as an extension of its core customer relationship management (CRM) solution. By leveraging its deep understanding of the industry and its existing client relationships, the company can introduce a complementary offering that addresses emerging market needs, driving organic growth through diversification.

Optimizing Internal Processes

In addition to capitalizing on existing capabilities and fostering innovation, organic growth strategies often involve the optimization of internal processes and systems. By streamlining operations, improving efficiency, and implementing best practices, businesses can achieve greater productivity, reduce costs, and free up resources to reinvest in growth initiatives.

For instance, a manufacturing company might implement lean production methods, automating certain processes and eliminating waste, enabling it to increase output and expand its customer base without the need for significant capital investments.

Expanding through Market Penetration

Organic growth strategies extend beyond the boundaries of a company's internal operations, also encompassing thoughtful market penetration and expansion initiatives.

Deepening Customer Relationships

One of the cornerstones of organic growth is the ability to deepen existing customer relationships. By understanding the evolving needs and preferences of their target audience, businesses can develop tailored solutions that foster loyalty and encourage repeat business.

A successful e-commerce retailer, for example, might introduce a personalized loyalty program that rewards customers for their continued patronage, offering exclusive discounts, early access to new products, and enhanced customer service. This approach not only strengthens the brand's connection with its current customer base but also serves as a powerful catalyst for organic growth through word-of-mouth and referrals.

Expanding into New Markets

While deepening customer relationships is crucial, organic growth strategies often involve strategic expansion into new markets, whether geographic or demographic. By carefully studying the competitive landscape, identifying underserved niches, and aligning product or service offerings with the unique needs of these new markets, businesses can cultivate sustainable growth without the need for drastic, capital-intensive moves.

Consider a global manufacturer of energy-efficient appliances that decides to enter a new international market. By conducting thorough market research, adapting its product lineup to local preferences, and establishing strategic partnerships with local distributors, the company can achieve organic growth through market expansion, without the risks associated with a full-scale acquisition or joint venture.

Diversifying the Product or Service Portfolio

Organic growth can also be driven by the strategic diversification of a company's product or service portfolio. By introducing complementary offerings that address the evolving needs of their existing customer base, businesses can unlock new revenue streams and position themselves as one-stop shops for their target market.

For instance, a financial services firm that started as an investment advisory practice may decide to expand its services to include wealth management, retirement planning, and insurance products. This diversification strategy allows the company to deepen its relationships with current clients while also attracting new customers seeking a comprehensive suite of financial solutions.

Cultivating a Culture of Sustainable Growth

Ultimately, the success of organic growth strategies lies in the cultivation of a corporate culture that embraces long-term, sustainable development. This involves instilling a mindset of continuous improvement, adaptability, and a deep understanding of the evolving market landscape.

Fostering Agility and Adaptability

In an environment of constant change, organic growth requires a nimble and adaptable approach. Businesses that encourage their teams to stay attuned to market trends, gather customer feedback, and quickly pivot in response to emerging opportunities or challenges are better positioned to capitalize on organic growth possibilities.

Investing in Employee Development

Organic growth strategies also rely on the expertise and dedication of a company's workforce. By investing in ongoing employee development, training, and skill-building initiatives, businesses can ensure that their teams possess the knowledge and capabilities required to drive innovation, optimize internal processes, and deliver exceptional customer experiences.

Cultivating a Collaborative Mindset

Organic growth often necessitates cross-functional collaboration, as teams from various departments come together to identify, evaluate, and execute growth opportunities. By fostering a culture of open communication, knowledge-sharing, and collective problem-solving, organizations can harness the collective intelligence of their workforce to fuel sustainable expansion.

In the pursuit of business growth, organic strategies offer a compelling alternative to more aggressive, capital-intensive approaches. By focusing on the optimization of internal strengths, thoughtful market penetration, and the cultivation of a growth-oriented corporate culture, companies can unlock sustainable expansion opportunities that align with their long-term vision and values. As the business landscape continues to evolve, the strategic application of organic growth principles will undoubtedly remain a key driver of success for savvy organizations.

Paid Advertising: When and How to Invest

In the dynamic world of modern marketing, paid advertising has emerged as a powerful tool for businesses of all sizes to reach their target audience and drive tangible results. Whether you're a startup looking to establish a foothold in the market or an established enterprise seeking to amplify your brand's visibility, understanding the intricacies of paid advertising can be the key to unlocking unprecedented growth.

When to Invest in Paid Advertising

The decision to invest in paid advertising should not be taken lightly, as it requires careful planning and a deep understanding of your business objectives. However, there are certain scenarios where paid advertising can be particularly beneficial:

1. **Launching a New Product or Service**: When introducing a new offering to the market, paid advertising can help you create awareness, generate interest, and drive initial sales. By strategically targeting your ads to reach the right audience, you can accelerate the adoption of your product or service and gain a competitive edge.

2. **Expanding into New Markets**: As your business ventures into new geographical regions or demographics, paid advertising can be an effective way to build brand recognition and reach potential customers who may not be familiar with your offerings. By tailoring your ad campaigns to the unique needs and preferences of these new markets, you can unlock untapped growth opportunities.

3. **Boosting Seasonal or Time-Sensitive Promotions**: Paid advertising can be particularly valuable when promoting limited-time offers, seasonal products, or time-sensitive events. By leveraging the immediacy and targeting capabilities of paid channels, you can effectively reach

your audience and drive conversions during these critical periods.

4. **Complementing Organic Marketing Efforts**: While organic marketing strategies, such as content creation and social media engagement, are essential for long-term brand building, paid advertising can amplify the reach and impact of these efforts. By strategically combining paid and organic tactics, you can maximize the visibility and effectiveness of your overall marketing strategy.

How to Invest in Paid Advertising

Investing in paid advertising requires a strategic approach that aligns with your business objectives and target audience. Here are some key steps to consider:

1. **Define Your Objectives**: Begin by clearly defining your goals for the paid advertising campaign, whether it's to increase brand awareness, drive website traffic, generate leads, or boost sales. Having a clear set of measurable objectives will help you allocate your resources effectively and track the success of your efforts.

2. **Identify Your Target Audience**: Thoroughly research your ideal customer profile, including their demographics, behaviors, interests, and pain points. This information will allow you to create targeted ad campaigns that resonate with your audience and increase the likelihood of conversion.

3. **Choose the Right Advertising Channels**: Depending on your target audience and campaign objectives, you may want to explore a variety of paid advertising channels, such as search engine advertising, social media advertising, display advertising, video advertising, or even traditional media like print or outdoor advertising. Evaluate the strengths and limitations of each channel to determine the most effective mix for your business.

4. **Develop Compelling Ad Creative**: Craft visually appealing and attention-grabbing ad creative that effectively communicates your value proposition and calls your audience to action. This may include eye-catching images, engaging videos, or concise and persuasive ad copy.

5. **Optimize and Iterate**: Continuously monitor the performance of your paid advertising campaigns, analyzing key metrics such as click-through rates, conversion rates, and return on investment (ROI). Use these insights to refine your targeting, messaging, and ad creativity, and make data-driven decisions to optimize the effectiveness of your campaigns over time.

6. **Measure and Analyze Results**: Implement robust tracking and analytics tools to measure the impact of your paid advertising efforts. This may include tracking website visitors, lead generation, sales, and other key performance indicators (KPIs) that align with your business objectives. By analyzing these metrics, you can gain valuable insights to guide future investment decisions and ensure a positive return on your advertising spend.

Paid advertising can be a powerful tool in your marketing arsenal, but it requires a strategic and data-driven approach to deliver meaningful results. By understanding the right time to invest and the key steps to effective paid advertising, you can unlock new avenues for growth, reach your target audience more effectively, and drive tangible business outcomes. Remember, the key to success lies in continuous optimization and a willingness to adapt your strategies based on the evolving needs of your customers and the changing landscape of the market.

Collaborations and Influencer Marketing

In today's digital landscape, collaborations, and influencer marketing have become powerful tools for businesses looking to expand their reach and connect with their target audience. These strategies leverage the power of partnerships and the influence of key individuals to drive brand awareness, engagement, and ultimately, sales.

Understanding Collaborations

Collaborations, in the context of marketing, involve two or more entities working together to create something unique or to promote each other's products or services. This could be a partnership between a brand and another brand, a brand, and an influencer, or even a brand and a non-profit organization. The key is to find complementary strengths and synergies that can benefit both parties involved.

Successful collaborations often result in increased visibility, access to new audiences, and the ability to create more engaging and memorable content. When executed well, collaborations can lead to a positive halo effect, where the reputations and positive associations of the involved parties are transferred to one another.

Exploring Influencer Marketing

Influencer marketing, on the other hand, focuses on leveraging the reach and credibility of individuals who have built a significant following in a particular niche or industry. These individuals, known as "influencers," have the power to sway the opinions and purchasing decisions of their followers.

By collaborating with relevant influencers, brands can tap into their audience's trust and gain access to a more engaged and targeted consumer base. Influencers can create sponsored content, promote products or services, or even serve as brand ambassadors, helping to amplify the brand's message and reach.

Strategies for Success

When it comes to collaborations and influencer marketing, there are several key strategies to consider:

1. **Identify the Right Partners**: Whether it's a brand or an influencer, it's crucial to carefully vet potential partners to ensure they align with your brand's values, target audience, and marketing objectives.

2. **Develop Meaningful Relationships**: Successful collaborations and influencer partnerships are built on mutual trust, respect, and a shared understanding of the goals and expectations.

3. **Create Authentic and Engaging Content**: Collaborations and influencer marketing should result in content that feels genuine and resonates with the target audience, rather than overtly promotional.

4. **Measure and Optimize**: Continuously track the performance of your collaborations and influencer marketing efforts, and be prepared to adjust your strategy as needed to achieve the best results.

By leveraging the power of collaborations and influencer marketing, businesses can unlock new growth opportunities, build stronger brand relationships, and stay ahead of the curve in the ever-evolving digital landscape.

Chapter 4

Engaging and Retaining Your Audience

Building Community: Interaction and Engagement

Cultivating a vibrant community is essential for any organization, whether it's a small business, a non-profit, or a global corporation. A thriving community fosters a sense of belonging, encourages collaboration, and drives innovation. At the heart of building a strong community lies the importance of interaction and engagement. By fostering meaningful connections and actively engaging with members, organizations can create a dynamic and inclusive environment that empowers individuals and propels the collective forward.

The Power of Interaction

Interaction is the lifeblood of a community. It is the catalyst for the exchange of ideas, the sharing of experiences, and the formation of meaningful relationships. When community members actively engage with one another, they cultivate a deeper understanding of each other's perspectives, challenges, and aspirations. This mutual understanding lays the foundation for trust, collaboration, and a shared sense of purpose.

Face-to-Face Engagement

While technology has revolutionized the way we communicate, there is still immense value in face-to-face interaction. Organizing in-person events, such as meetups, workshops, or social gatherings, provides community members with the opportunity to connect on a personal level. These face-to-face interactions allow for the exchange of nonverbal cues, the fostering of genuine connections, and the creation of lasting memories that strengthen the bonds within the community.

Online Interaction

In today's digital landscape, online interaction has become a vital component of building community. Platforms like discussion forums, social media, and collaborative tools enable community members to engage with one another regardless of geographical barriers. These digital spaces allow for the rapid dissemination of information, the formation of special interest groups, and the facilitation of real-time discussions on topics that matter to the community.

Fostering Engagement

Engagement is the cornerstone of a thriving community. It is the active participation and investment of community members in the collective experience. By cultivating a culture of engagement, organizations can inspire their members to contribute, share, and collaborate in meaningful ways.

Encouraging Participation

One of the key strategies for fostering engagement is to encourage active participation from community members. This can be achieved through a variety of methods, such as:

- Hosting regular events or activities that cater to the diverse interests of the community

- Inviting members to share their expertise, experiences, or creative work

- Providing opportunities for members to volunteer or take on leadership roles within the community

- Recognizing and celebrating the contributions of engaged community members

Facilitating Collaboration

Collaboration is a powerful driver of engagement within a community. When members work together towards a common goal, they cultivate a sense of shared purpose and investment in the community's success. Organizations can facilitate collaboration by:

- Establishing collaborative workspaces or project-based initiatives

- Encouraging the formation of special interest groups or task forces

- Facilitating the exchange of knowledge and best practices among community members

Empowering Community Leadership

Empowering community members to take on leadership roles is another effective way to foster engagement. By providing opportunities for individuals to become actively involved in the community's decision-making and direction, organizations can:

- Tap into the diverse talents and insights of the community

- Cultivate a sense of ownership and investment among community members

- Develop a self-sustaining ecosystem where members take initiative and drive the community's growth

Measuring and Improving Engagement

To ensure the ongoing success of a community, it is essential to measure and continuously improve engagement levels. This can be achieved through:

- Gathering feedback from community members through surveys, interviews, or focus groups

- Analyzing engagement metrics, such as participation rates, content sharing, and member retention

- Identifying areas for improvement and implementing strategies to address them

By consistently monitoring and refining their engagement efforts, organizations can maintain a vibrant and thriving community that continues to meet the evolving needs of its members.

Building a strong community through interaction and engagement is a transformative process that can have far-reaching benefits for organizations and their members. By fostering meaningful connections, facilitating collaboration, and empowering community leadership, organizations can create an environment that inspires individuals to contribute, grow, and thrive together. As communities continue to evolve in the digital age, the principles of interaction and engagement will remain at the core of building resilient, inclusive, and impactful communities.

Customer Service Through Social Media

Social media platforms have become an integral part of our daily lives, with billions of people worldwide actively using platforms like Facebook, Twitter, Instagram, and LinkedIn. This ubiquitous presence of social media has made it a crucial channel for businesses to connect with their customers.

One of the primary advantages of leveraging social media for customer service is the ability to respond to queries and address concerns promptly. Customers today expect immediate responses, and social media enables businesses to provide quick resolutions to issues, fostering a sense of trust and loyalty.

Moreover, social media platforms allow businesses to proactively engage with their customers, addressing their needs and concerns before they escalate. By monitoring social media conversations, businesses can identify potential problems and address them promptly, preventing small issues from becoming larger ones.

Enhancing Customer Experiences through Social Media

Beyond simply responding to customer inquiries, businesses can use social media to enhance the overall customer experience. By crafting engaging content, businesses can build stronger relationships with their customers, showcasing their brand personality and values.

For instance, businesses can use social media to share behind-the-scenes glimpses of their operations, introduce their team members, or celebrate customer milestones. This level of transparency and personalization can help customers feel more connected to the brand, fostering a sense of loyalty and advocacy.

Furthermore, social media platforms offer businesses the opportunity to gather valuable customer feedback and insights. By encouraging customers to share their thoughts, opinions, and suggestions, businesses can gain a deeper understanding of their needs and preferences, allowing them to make informed decisions and continuously improve their products or services.

Effective Strategies for Social Media Customer Service

Implementing an effective social media customer service strategy requires a thoughtful and strategic approach. Here are some key considerations:

1. **Responsiveness**: Customers expect prompt responses to their inquiries and concerns. Businesses should have a dedicated team or process in place to monitor social media channels and respond to customers promptly.

2. **Personalization**: Avoid generic, one-size-fits-all responses. Instead, personalize interactions by addressing customers by name and tailoring the tone and language to each individual.

3. **Consistency**: Ensure that the customer service experience is consistent across all social media channels. Customers should receive the same level of care and attention regardless of the platform they choose to engage with.

4. **Empowerment**: Empower your customer service team to make informed decisions and take decisive actions to resolve customer issues. This can help build trust and foster stronger relationships.

5. **Continuous Improvement**: Regularly analyze customer feedback and social media metrics to identify areas for improvement. Use this data to refine your social media customer service strategies and enhance the overall customer experience.

In the age of digital transformation, social media has become an indispensable tool for businesses to provide exceptional customer service. By embracing the power of social media, businesses can build stronger, more personalized relationships with their customers, address their concerns in real time, and continuously improve the overall customer experience.

As the landscape of customer service continues to evolve, businesses that prioritize social media as a key component of their customer service strategy will be well-positioned to thrive and maintain a competitive edge in the years to come.

Monitoring and Responding to Feedback

Effective communication is the cornerstone of any successful endeavor, whether it's a business venture, a personal project, or a collaborative effort. At the heart of this communication lies the ability to monitor and respond to feedback - a critical skill that enables us to navigate the complexities of the modern world and drive meaningful progress.

In today's fast-paced and ever-evolving landscape, the ability to listen, analyze, and act on feedback is essential. It allows us to stay attuned to the needs and concerns of our stakeholders, whether they are clients, colleagues, or the wider community. By monitoring and responding to feedback, we can gain invaluable insights that inform our decision-making, refine our strategies, and ultimately, ensure that our efforts are aligned with the needs and expectations of those we serve.

One of the key benefits of monitoring and responding to feedback is the opportunity to identify and address pain points or areas for improvement. When we actively solicit and analyze feedback, we become better equipped to pinpoint the challenges or obstacles that may be hindering progress or causing frustration. By addressing these issues promptly and effectively, we can enhance the overall experience and build stronger, more trusting relationships with our stakeholders.

Moreover, monitoring and responding to feedback can also serve as a powerful catalyst for innovation and growth. By understanding the evolving needs and preferences of our audience, we can identify emerging trends, anticipate new opportunities, and develop innovative solutions that create lasting value. This agility and adaptability are critical in today's rapidly changing business environment, where the ability to pivot and respond to market shifts can mean the difference between success and failure.

Effective feedback monitoring and response also foster a culture of continuous improvement and accountability. By actively seeking out and incorporating feedback, we demonstrate our commitment to ongoing learning and development, both at the individual and organizational levels. This, in turn, can inspire a sense of ownership and engagement among our stakeholders, as they feel heard and empowered to contribute to the overall success of the endeavor.

Implementing a robust feedback monitoring and response system requires a multifaceted approach. It begins with establishing clear communication channels and mechanisms for gathering feedback, such as surveys, focus groups, or online platforms. By making it easy and accessible for stakeholders to share their thoughts and experiences, we can ensure that we are capturing a diverse and representative range of perspectives.

Once the feedback has been collected, the next step is to analyze it systematically, identifying patterns, trends, and areas of concern. This process may involve the use of data analysis tools, qualitative coding, or collaborative workshops, all to distill the most meaningful and actionable insights.

Armed with these insights, the final step is to formulate a thoughtful and responsive action plan. This may involve implementing changes to products, services, or processes, addressing specific concerns raised by stakeholders, or communicating the steps being taken to address the feedback.

Importantly, it is essential to close the loop by providing timely updates and feedback on the actions taken, demonstrating a genuine commitment to continuous improvement.

Monitoring and responding to feedback is not a one-time event, but rather an ongoing, iterative process that requires dedication, empathy, and a willingness to learn and adapt. By embracing this approach, we can foster a culture of continuous improvement, drive innovation, and build stronger, more trusting relationships with our stakeholders - all of which are essential ingredients for long-term success and sustainability.

In conclusion, the ability to monitor and respond to feedback is a fundamental skill in today's rapidly changing world. By actively seeking out and incorporating the perspectives and experiences of our stakeholders, we can unlock new opportunities, address pressing challenges, and ultimately, create a more meaningful and impactful path forward. It is a skill that transcends industries and disciplines, and one that, when mastered, can propel us towards greater success and fulfillment.

Creating Loyalty Programs and Incentives

In today's highly competitive business landscape, customer loyalty has become a crucial factor in determining a company's long-term success. Businesses that can cultivate a loyal customer base can enjoy a multitude of benefits, from steady revenue streams to increased word-of-mouth marketing and brand advocacy. One of the most effective strategies for building and maintaining customer loyalty is the implementation of well-designed loyalty programs and incentives.

Defining Customer Loyalty

Before delving into the intricacies of loyalty programs and incentives, it's important to understand the concept of customer loyalty itself. Customer loyalty is the deep commitment a customer has towards a brand, product, or service, which manifests in their consistent and repeated patronage. Loyal customers are not only more likely to make repeat purchases, but they are also more willing to recommend the brand to their friends and family and are generally less price-sensitive than their less loyal counterparts.

The Benefits of Customer Loyalty

Fostering customer loyalty can provide a myriad of benefits for businesses of all sizes and industries. Some of the most significant advantages include:

1. **Increased Revenue**: Loyal customers tend to spend more on a brand's products or services, leading to higher revenue and profitability.

2. **Reduced Marketing Costs**: Loyal customers are more likely to engage in word-of-mouth marketing, effectively reducing the need for expensive advertising and promotional campaigns.

3. **Enhanced Brand Reputation**: Loyal customers can serve as brand ambassadors, further strengthening the company's reputation and credibility in the eyes of potential new customers.

4. **Improved Customer Retention**: Retaining existing customers is generally more cost-effective than acquiring

new ones, and loyal customers are less likely to churn or switch to a competitor.

Designing Effective Loyalty Programs

Crafting a successful loyalty program requires a deep understanding of your target audience and their motivations. Effective loyalty programs are built upon the following key principles:

1. **Simplicity**: The program should be easy to understand and navigate, with clear and transparent rules and benefits.

2. **Relevance**: The rewards and incentives offered should be aligned with the preferences and needs of your target customers, making the program genuinely valuable to them.

3. **Personalization**: Tailoring the program to individual customer preferences and behaviors can enhance its perceived value and engagement.

4. **Consistency**: Maintaining a consistent and reliable loyalty program experience can foster a sense of trust and commitment among customers.

5. **Emotional Connection**: Successful loyalty programs often incorporate elements that create an emotional bond between the customer and the brand, such as VIP experiences or exclusive perks.

Incentives and Rewards

The backbone of any effective loyalty program is a well-designed system of incentives and rewards. These can take many forms, including:

1. **Point-based Systems**: Customers earn points for every purchase or engagement, which can be redeemed for various rewards or discounts.

2. **Tier-based Programs**: Customers are assigned to different tiers based on their spending or engagement levels, with higher tiers unlocking more exclusive or valuable rewards.

3. **Experiential Rewards**: Offering unique experiences, such as exclusive events or VIP treatment, can create a sense of exclusivity and heighten the emotional connection with the brand.

4. **Personalized Rewards**: Tailoring rewards to individual customer preferences and behaviors can make the program feel more meaningful and valuable.

5. **Partnerships and Cross-Promotions**: Collaborating with complementary brands or businesses to offer a broader range of rewards can enhance the program's appeal and perceived value.

Measuring and Optimizing Loyalty Programs

Effective loyalty programs require ongoing monitoring and optimization to ensure they continue to deliver value to both the business and the customers. Key metrics to track include:

1. **Participation Rates**: The percentage of customers actively engaged with the loyalty program.

2. **Redemption Rates**: The rate at which customers are redeeming their earned rewards or incentives.

3. **Customer Lifetime Value**: The total revenue generated from a customer throughout their relationship with the brand.

4. **Customer Retention Rates**: The percentage of customers who continue to do business with the company over time.

5. **Net Promoter Score**: A measure of customer loyalty and willingness to recommend the brand to others.

By continuously analyzing these metrics and adjusting the program accordingly, businesses can ensure that their loyalty initiatives remain effective and relevant in the ever-evolving market.

In today's competitive business environment, the ability to cultivate and maintain a loyal customer base can be the difference between success and failure. By designing and implementing effective loyalty programs and incentives, businesses can not only boost their revenue and profitability but also strengthen their brand reputation and create a sustainable competitive advantage. By keeping the principles of simplicity, relevance, personalization, and emotional connection at the forefront, companies can build loyalty programs that truly resonate with their customers and drive long-term growth.

Chapter 5

Measuring Success and Making Adjustments

Key Metrics to Track for social media marketing

In the ever-evolving landscape of digital marketing, social media has become an indispensable tool for businesses of all sizes. It provides a powerful platform to connect with your target audience, build brand awareness, and drive conversions. However, to truly maximize the impact of your social media efforts, it's crucial to identify and track the right key metrics. The essential metrics you should monitor to ensure the success of your social media marketing strategy.

Audience Growth

One of the fundamental metrics to track is your audience growth across your social media channels. This includes metrics such as:

- ➢ **Followers/Fans**: The total number of people who have chosen to follow your brand on a specific platform. This metric indicates the size of your potential reach and engagement.

- ➢ **New Followers**: The number of new people who have started following your brand over a given period. This metric allows you to gauge the effectiveness of your content and outreach efforts in attracting new followers.

- **Follower Growth Rate**: The rate at which your follower count is increasing or decreasing. This metric can help you assess the overall health and momentum of your social media presence.

Monitoring these audience metrics can provide valuable insights into the success of your social media strategy and help you identify areas for improvement.

Engagement

Engagement is a crucial metric that measures the level of interaction and connection your audience has with your content. Some key engagement metrics to track include:

- **Likes/Reactions**: The number of times your content has been liked or reacted to by your followers. This metric indicates the level of interest and approval your content is receiving.

- **Comments**: The number of comments left on your posts. This metric reflects the level of dialogue and active engagement your content is generating.

- **Shares/Retweets**: The number of times your content has been shared or retweeted by your followers. This metric showcases the shareability and virality of your content.

- **Click-Through Rate (CTR)**: The ratio of users who click on a specific link or call to action within your social media content. This metric can help you assess the effectiveness of your content in driving desired actions.

By monitoring these engagement metrics, you can gain insights into the types of content that resonate most with your audience and make data-driven decisions to optimize your social media strategy.

Reach and Impressions

Reach and impressions are crucial metrics that measure the visibility and exposure of your social media content. These include:

- **Reach**: The total number of unique users who have seen your content. This metric provides insight into the overall visibility of your posts.

- **Impressions**: The total number of times your content has been displayed, including multiple views by the same user. This metric can help you gauge the overall exposure and potential impact of your content.

Tracking reach and impressions can help you understand the effectiveness of your content distribution and identify opportunities to increase your visibility on social media platforms.

Conversion and ROI

Ultimately, the success of your social media marketing efforts should be measured by their ability to drive tangible business results. Key metrics to track in this regard include:

- **Conversions**: The number of users who have taken a desired action, such as making a purchase, signing up for a newsletter, or filling out a lead form. This metric directly ties your social media efforts to your business objectives.

- **Return on Investment (ROI)**: The ratio of the revenue or value generated from your social media marketing efforts to the cost of those efforts. This metric helps you evaluate the overall effectiveness and profitability of your social media strategy.

By tracking conversion and ROI metrics, you can demonstrate the tangible impact of your social media marketing on your business and make data-driven decisions to optimize your investment.

Monitoring and Analyzing

To effectively track and analyze these key metrics, it's essential to have a comprehensive social media analytics tool or platform. These tools can provide detailed insights and visualizations to help you make sense of your data.

Additionally, it's important to regularly review and analyze your metrics, identify trends, and make adjustments to your social media strategy accordingly. This iterative process will help you continuously improve the effectiveness of your social media marketing efforts and achieve your desired business goals.

Focusing on the key metrics outlined in this guide, you can gain a deep understanding of your social media performance, make informed decisions, and drive real business results. Remember, social media marketing is a dynamic and ever-evolving field, so stay agile, and adaptable, and always strive to learn and improve.

Tools and Analytics for Social Media

In the ever-evolving digital landscape, social media has become a fundamental tool for businesses and individuals alike. As the influence and reach of social platforms continue to grow, the need for effective tools and analytical insights has become increasingly crucial. The various tools and analytics available to help you navigate the complex world of social media and maximize your online presence.

Understanding the Social Media Landscape

Before delving into the specific tools and analytics, it's essential to have a solid grasp of the social media landscape. Different platforms cater to different audiences, offer unique features, and present unique opportunities for engagement. From the visual-driven Instagram to the professional networking site LinkedIn, each platform requires a tailored approach to effectively connect with your target audience.

Choosing the Right Social Media Tools

With the abundance of social media tools available, it can be overwhelming to determine which ones are best suited for your needs. The key is to identify the specific goals you aim to achieve, whether it's increased brand awareness, lead generation, or customer engagement. Some of the most widely used tools in the social media arsenal include:

1. **Content Scheduling and Management**: Tools like Hootsuite, Buffer, and Sprout Social allow you to plan, schedule, and automate your social media posts across

multiple platforms, ensuring a consistent and strategic presence.

2. **Social Media Listening**: Tools such as Mention, Talkwalker, and Brandwatch enable you to monitor conversations, track brand mentions, and identify potential opportunities or challenges in real time.

3. **Influencer Identification and Outreach**: Platforms like BuzzSumo and Upfluence help you identify influential individuals within your industry, assess their reach and engagement, and facilitate collaborative partnerships.

4. **Social Media Analytics**: Tools like Google Analytics, Facebook Insights, and Twitter Analytics provide invaluable data on your audience demographics, content performance, and overall social media effectiveness.

Leveraging Social Media Analytics

The true power of social media lies in the wealth of data and insights it provides. By utilizing robust analytics tools, you can gain a deeper understanding of your audience, optimize your content strategy, and measure the impact of your social media efforts.

1. **Audience Insights**: Analyze your follower demographics, interests, and behaviors to create targeted content that resonates with your audience.

2. **Content Performance**: Evaluate which types of posts, formats, and content themes perform best, and use this information to refine your content strategy.

3. **Engagement Metrics**: Track likes, comments, shares, and other engagement metrics to gauge the effectiveness of your social media campaigns and identify areas for improvement.

4. **Competitive Analysis**: Benchmark your social media performance against industry peers and competitors to identify opportunities for growth and differentiation.

5. **Conversion Tracking**: Integrate your social media platforms with e-commerce or lead-generation tools to measure the direct impact of your social media efforts on your business objectives.

Optimizing Your Social Media Strategy

Armed with the right tools and analytical insights, you can continuously refine and optimize your social media strategy. This includes:

1. **Content Curation and Creation**: Leverage data-driven insights to create high-performing content that resonates with your audience.

2. **Audience Targeting and Segmentation**: Use advanced targeting options to reach the right people at the right time with personalized messaging.

3. **Paid Social Media Advertising**: Utilize targeted paid campaigns to amplify your organic social media efforts and achieve specific business goals.

4. **Collaboration and Influencer Marketing**: Identify and collaborate with relevant industry influencers to tap into their established audiences and boost your brand's credibility.

5. **Continuous Optimization**: Regularly review your social media analytics, test new approaches, and make data-driven adjustments to your strategy.

In the dynamic world of social media, the right tools and analytics can be the key to unlocking your full potential. By understanding the landscape, selecting the appropriate tools, and leveraging data-driven insights, you can effectively navigate the social media maze and achieve your desired business objectives. Embrace the power of social media analytics and embark on a journey of continuous optimization and growth.

A/B Testing: What It Is and Why It Matters

A/B testing, also known as split testing, is a powerful tool for optimizing digital experiences and making data-driven decisions. It involves comparing two versions of a webpage, app, or marketing campaign to determine which performs better. By systematically testing different variations, businesses can uncover insights that lead to higher conversions, increased engagement, and improved user satisfaction.

Understanding A/B Testing

At its core, A/B testing is a method of comparing two or more versions of a digital element to see which one performs better. This could be anything from a landing page, an email subject line, a product image, or a call-to-action button. The process involves creating a control version (A) and one or more variations (B, C, D, etc.) and then directing a percentage of your traffic to each version.

The key is to ensure that the only difference between the versions is the element you're testing. This allows you to isolate the impact of that specific change and draw clear conclusions about its effectiveness. By analyzing the performance metrics, such as conversion rates, click-through rates, or time spent on the page, you can determine which version resonates better with your audience.

The Benefits of A/B Testing

Implementing A/B testing in your digital strategy can provide numerous benefits for your business:

1. **Optimization**: A/B testing enables you to continually refine and improve your digital assets, ensuring that you're providing the best possible experience for your customers. Even small changes, such as the color of a button or the placement of an image, can have a significant impact on user behavior and conversion rates.

2. **Data-Driven Decisions**: Rather than relying on assumptions or gut feelings, A/B testing allows you to make decisions based on actual user data. This helps you

avoid costly mistakes and ensures that you're investing your resources in the most effective solutions.

3. **Increased Conversions**: By identifying the variations that perform better, you can implement the winning version and enjoy a boost in conversions, whether that's sales, leads, sign-ups, or any other desired action.

4. **Improved User Experience**: A/B testing helps you understand your audience's preferences and expectations, allowing you to tailor your digital experiences to better meet their needs. This can lead to higher engagement, loyalty, and customer satisfaction.

5. **Reduced Risks**: By testing different ideas and hypotheses before fully implementing them, A/B testing helps you mitigate the risks associated with making changes to your digital assets. You can experiment with new concepts without jeopardizing your existing performance.

6. **Scalable Optimization**: As your business grows and your digital presence expands, A/B testing becomes an invaluable tool for managing and optimizing multiple touchpoints across your customer journey. It allows you to continuously refine and improve your digital strategy at scale.

Implementing A/B Testing

Implementing A/B testing in your business involves several key steps:

1. **Define Your Goals**: Clearly define what you want to achieve with your A/B test, whether it's increasing sales, improving user engagement, or enhancing the overall customer experience.

2. **Identify the Element to Test**: Determine the specific element or feature you want to test, such as a call-to-action, product image, or page layout.

3. **Create Variations**: Develop the control version (A) and one or more variations (B, C, D, etc.) that differ only in the element you're testing.

4. **Set Up the Test**: Use a specialized A/B testing tool or platform to set up the test and allocate traffic to each version.

5. **Monitor and Analyze**: Closely monitor the performance of each version and analyze the results to determine the winning variation.

6. **Implement the Winner**: Once you've identified the better-performing version, implement it across your digital assets and continue to test new ideas for further optimization.

A/B testing is a powerful tool that enables businesses to make data-driven decisions and continuously improve their digital experiences. By systematically testing different variations, you can uncover valuable insights and implement changes that lead to higher conversions, increased engagement, and enhanced user satisfaction. Embracing A/B testing as a core part of your digital strategy can help you stay ahead of the competition and deliver exceptional results for your business.

Adapting Strategies Based on Performance Data

As the business landscape continues to evolve, organizations must be agile and responsive to remain competitive. One of the key ways to achieve this is by closely monitoring and analyzing performance data to inform strategic decision-making. By adapting strategies based on this data, companies can maximize their chances of success and stay ahead of the curve.

Understanding the Importance of Performance Data

Performance data is the lifeblood of any organization. It provides valuable insights into the effectiveness of current strategies, the impact of new initiatives, and the overall health of the business. This information can come from a variety of sources, such as sales figures, customer feedback, website analytics, and financial reports.

By closely analyzing this data, leaders can identify areas of strength and weakness, uncover emerging trends, and make informed decisions about where to allocate resources. This allows them to refine their strategies and adapt to changing market conditions, ensuring that their efforts are aligned with the needs and preferences of their target audience.

Developing a Data-Driven Mindset

Adapting strategies based on performance data requires a fundamental shift in mindset. Instead of relying solely on instinct or experience, organizations must embrace a data-driven approach to decision-making. This means:

1. **Establishing Clear Metrics**: Identify the key performance indicators (KPIs) that are most relevant to your business goals. These could include sales figures, customer satisfaction scores, website traffic, or any other metrics that provide meaningful insights into your organization's performance.

2. **Collecting and Organizing Data**: Implement robust data collection and management systems to ensure that you have access to accurate, up-to-date information. This may involve integrating various software platforms, automating data-gathering processes, and establishing clear data governance protocols.

3. **Analyzing and Interpreting Data**: Develop the skills and tools necessary to analyze performance data effectively. This could involve using data visualization tools, conducting statistical analyses, or seeking the expertise of data analysts or data scientists.

4. **Communicating Insights**: Ensure that the insights derived from performance data are communicated effectively to relevant stakeholders, from frontline employees to senior leadership. This will help to foster a data-driven culture and empower decision-makers at all levels of the organization.

Adapting Strategies in Response to Performance Data

Once you have a solid understanding of your organization's performance data, the next step is to use this information to adapt your strategies. This process can be broken down into several key steps:

1. **Identify Areas for Improvement**: Carefully review your performance data to pinpoint areas where your current strategies are falling short. This could be a decline in sales, a drop in customer satisfaction, or a lack of engagement on your digital platforms.

2. **Hypothesize Potential Solutions**: Based on your analysis, generate a list of hypothetical solutions or adjustments that could address the identified issues. This may involve tweaking marketing campaigns, revising product offerings, or modifying operational processes.

3. **Test and Evaluate**: Implement small-scale tests or pilots to assess the effectiveness of your proposed solutions. Closely monitor the results and be prepared to make further adjustments as necessary.

4. **Scale Successful Strategies**: Once you've identified successful strategies, work to scale them across your organization. This may involve expanding the reach of successful campaigns, replicating effective operational processes, or implementing new technologies to support the scaled efforts.

5. **Continuously Refine**: Ongoing monitoring and analysis of performance data is essential. As market conditions and customer needs evolve, you must be prepared to make further adjustments to your strategies to maintain a competitive edge.

Overcoming Challenges and Fostering a Data-Driven Culture

Adapting strategies based on performance data is not without its challenges. Some common obstacles include:

- **Resistance to Change**: Employees may be reluctant to embrace a data-driven approach, preferring to rely on traditional methods or personal intuition.

- **Data Quality and Availability**: Ensuring the accuracy, completeness, and timeliness of performance data can be a significant challenge, especially for organizations with legacy systems or siloed data.

- **Analytical Capabilities**: Developing the necessary skills and tools to effectively analyze and interpret performance data may require significant investment in training and technology.

To overcome these challenges, organizations must foster a strong data-driven culture that emphasizes the importance of continuous learning, innovation, and collaboration. This may involve:

- **Providing Data Literacy Training**: Equipping employees at all levels with the skills and knowledge to understand and interpret performance data.

- **Encouraging Data-Driven Decision-Making**: Empowering employees to use data to inform their decision-making processes and to challenge established assumptions.

- **Investing in Data Infrastructure**: Upgrading data management systems, integrating analytics tools, and ensuring data quality and accessibility.

- **Celebrating Data-Driven Success Stories**: Highlighting examples of how data-driven strategies have led to successful outcomes, and using these as inspiration for further innovation.

By embracing a data-driven mindset and continuously adapting their strategies in response to performance data, organizations can position themselves for long-term success in an increasingly competitive and rapidly changing business landscape.

Chapter 6

Advanced Tactics and Future Trends

The Role of AI and Automation in Social Media

In the ever-evolving landscape of social media, the impact of artificial intelligence (AI) and automation has become increasingly profound. As the digital world continues to expand, these technological advancements have transformed the way we create, share, and engage with content on various social platforms.

The Rise of AI-Powered Content Creation

One of the most significant ways AI has influenced social media is in the realm of content creation. Intelligent algorithms and machine learning models have empowered users to generate content at unprecedented speeds and scale. From automatically captioning images to generating personalized captions and even complete posts, AI has revolutionized the content creation process.

This automation has enabled individuals and businesses to amplify their social media presence, ensuring a constant stream of fresh and engaging content. However, this shift has also raised concerns about the authenticity and quality of user-generated content. As AI-powered tools become more sophisticated, the line between human-created and machine-generated content can become blurred, leading to potential issues with trust and transparency.

Personalized User Experiences

Another key aspect of AI's influence on social media is the ability to deliver highly personalized user experiences. Through advanced data analysis and machine learning algorithms, social media platforms can now tailor content, recommendations, and even advertising to each user's preferences and behaviors.

This level of personalization has significantly improved the user experience, as individuals are more likely to engage with content that is relevant and appealing to them. By understanding user interests, preferences, and habits, social media platforms can create more immersive and engaging experiences, ultimately fostering stronger connections between users and the brands or communities they interact with.

Intelligent Content Curation and Recommendation

In addition to personalized experiences, AI has also revolutionized the way social media platforms curate and recommend content to users. Sophisticated algorithms analyze vast amounts of data, including user interactions, content performance, and emerging trends, to identify the most relevant and engaging content for each individual.

This intelligent curation and recommendation system have transformed the way users discover new content and connect with others on social media. By surfacing the most compelling and relevant information, AI-powered content curation has the potential to enhance the overall user experience and foster more meaningful interactions.

Automated Moderation and Content Moderation

As social media platforms have grown in size and complexity, the challenge of moderating user-generated content has become increasingly daunting. Here, too, AI and automation have played a crucial role in helping platforms manage and moderate content at scale.

Through the use of natural language processing, image recognition, and other AI-driven techniques, social media platforms can now automatically detect and flag potentially harmful or inappropriate content. This automated moderation process has enabled platforms to respond to violations and mitigate the spread of misinformation, hate speech, and other problematic content more efficiently.

However, the reliance on AI-powered moderation has also raised concerns about the potential for errors, biases, and the need for human oversight to ensure the fair and ethical treatment of user-generated content.

The Impact on Social Media Marketers and Businesses

The integration of AI and automation in social media has had a significant impact on the way businesses and marketers approach their digital strategies. From the ability to create targeted and personalized campaigns to the use of AI-powered analytics and optimization tools, these technologies have transformed the landscape of social media marketing.

Businesses can now leverage AI to gain deeper insights into their audience, identify the most effective content and messaging, and optimize their social media campaigns for maximum impact. Automated scheduling, content curation, and performance tracking have streamlined the workflow of social media marketers, allowing them to focus on more strategic and creative aspects of their campaigns.

Ethical Considerations and the Future of AI in Social Media

As the role of AI and automation in social media continues to evolve, it is essential to consider the ethical implications and potential challenges that may arise. Issues such as data privacy, algorithmic bias, and the impact on user well-being must be carefully addressed to ensure that the benefits of these technologies are realized while minimizing their potential for harm.

Moving forward, social media platforms, policymakers, and the wider public must engage in an ongoing dialogue about the responsible and ethical use of AI and automation. This will involve developing robust governance frameworks, transparency measures, and user-centric policies to safeguard the integrity and well-being of social media ecosystems.

The integration of AI and automation in social media has transformed the way we create, consume, and interact with content. From personalized user experiences to intelligent content curation and automated moderation, these technologies have revolutionized the social media landscape.

As we navigate the ever-evolving digital world, it is essential to continue exploring the benefits and challenges of AI and automation in social media, ensuring that these powerful tools are leveraged in a manner that fosters meaningful connections, protects user privacy, and maintains the integrity of social media platforms. By striking the right balance between technological innovation and ethical responsibility, we can harness the full potential of AI and automation to enhance the social media experience for all.

Exploring Emerging Platforms and Features

In the ever-evolving landscape of technology, the emergence of new platforms and features is a constant source of excitement and innovation. It's crucial to understand and embrace these advancements, as they hold the potential to transform the way we interact with the digital world.

The Rise of Immersive Experiences

One of the most captivating developments in recent years has been the rapid progression of virtual and augmented reality technologies. These platforms offer users an unparalleled level of immersion, blurring the lines between the physical and digital realms.

From virtual gaming experiences that transport players to fantastical worlds to augmented reality applications that seamlessly integrate digital elements into our everyday lives, these technologies are redefining the way we perceive and engage with information.

As these platforms continue to evolve, they are opening up new avenues for entertainment, education, and even e-commerce, allowing businesses and individuals to create more engaging and interactive experiences for their audiences.

The Power of Artificial Intelligence

Artificial Intelligence (AI) has emerged as a transformative force, revolutionizing various industries and aspects of our lives. From intelligent personal assistants that anticipate our needs to sophisticated machine learning algorithms that analyze vast amounts of data, AI is helping us streamline tasks, make more informed decisions, and unlock new levels of productivity.

One of the most exciting developments in the realm of AI is the rapid advancement of natural language processing (NLP). NLP enables machines to understand, interpret, and generate human language, allowing for more intuitive and conversational interactions. This technology is powering the rise of chatbots, virtual assistants, and language translation services, making communication across barriers more seamless than ever before.

As AI continues to evolve, we can expect to see its influence expand even further, with potential applications in fields such as healthcare, transportation, and even creative pursuits. The key to harnessing the power of AI lies in understanding its capabilities and ensuring that it is developed and deployed ethically and responsibly.

The Proliferation of Mobile Platforms

The ubiquity of smartphones and mobile devices has transformed the way we access information, communicate, and engage with the world around us. Mobile platforms have become the gateway to a wealth of content, services, and experiences, revolutionizing the way we work, learn, and entertain ourselves.

One of the most significant advancements in mobile technology has been the rise of progressive web applications (PWAs). PWAs combine the best features of traditional web pages and native mobile apps, offering users a seamless and responsive experience regardless of the device they're using. This technology has the potential to bridge the gap between web and mobile, providing businesses with a more efficient and cost-effective way to reach their audiences.

In addition to PWAs, the growing ecosystem of mobile apps continues to expand, with innovative features and capabilities that cater to an ever-widening range of user needs. From productivity tools and fitness trackers to social media and entertainment platforms, the mobile app landscape is a constantly evolving space that is shaping our daily digital experiences.

The Emergence of the Internet of Things

The Internet of Things (IoT) is another exciting development that is transforming the way we interact with the world around us. This network of interconnected devices, sensors, and appliances is enabling new levels of automation, optimization, and data-driven insights.

From smart home systems that allow us to control our environments remotely, to wearable devices that monitor our health and fitness, the IoT is creating a more connected and responsive world. As these technologies become more widespread, they have the potential to enhance our quality of life, improve energy efficiency, and streamline various aspects of our daily routines.

Moreover, the data generated by IoT devices can be leveraged by businesses and researchers to gain valuable insights, inform decision-making, and develop innovative solutions to address real-world challenges.

Embracing the Future

As we navigate this rapidly changing technological landscape, it's essential to approach these emerging platforms and features with an open and curious mindset. By embracing the opportunities presented by these advancements, we can unlock new avenues for personal and professional growth, enhance our quality of life, and contribute to the ongoing progress of our digital world.

Whether it's immersing ourselves in virtual experiences, harnessing the power of AI, optimizing our mobile workflows, or integrating smart devices into our daily lives, the future is filled with possibilities. By staying informed, adaptable, and proactive, we can position ourselves to thrive in this ever-evolving digital era.

Staying Ahead: Trends to Watch in Social Media Marketing

In the ever-evolving landscape of digital marketing, social media has emerged as a dominant force, transforming the way businesses engage with their customers and build their brands. As we move forward, marketers must stay ahead of the curve and anticipate the emerging trends that will shape the future of social media marketing.

One of the most significant trends to watch in the social media landscape is the continued rise of video content. With platforms like TikTok, Instagram Reels, and YouTube Shorts capturing the attention of users worldwide, the demand for visually engaging, short-form video content has skyrocketed. Businesses that adapt to this trend and incorporate more videos into their social media strategies will be well-positioned to connect with their audience in a more impactful and memorable way.

Moreover, the integration of augmented reality (AR) and virtual reality (VR) technologies into social media platforms is another trend that savvy marketers should have on their radar. As users become increasingly immersed in these interactive experiences, brands can leverage AR and VR to create unique, engaging content that stands out in the crowded social media landscape. From virtual product try-ons to immersive brand experiences, the possibilities are endless for businesses that embrace these cutting-edge technologies.

Another trend that is gaining momentum in the social media sphere is the growing importance of influencer marketing. As consumers become more skeptical of traditional advertising, they are turning to trusted social media personalities to guide their purchasing decisions. By partnering with influential individuals who align with their brand values and target audience, businesses can tap into the power of authentic, word-of-mouth marketing to reach new customers and build brand loyalty.

However, the landscape of influencer marketing is continuously evolving, and savvy marketers must stay ahead of the curve to ensure their collaborations are effective and impactful. This might involve exploring micro-influencers or nano-influencers, who often boast highly engaged and loyal followings, or leveraging the power of user-generated content and social proof to amplify their brand message.

The rise of social commerce is another trend that is transforming the way businesses approach social media marketing. With the integration of e-commerce capabilities directly within social media platforms, consumers can now seamlessly discover, research, and purchase products without ever leaving the comfort of their favorite social apps. By optimizing their social media presence for shoppable content and creating a frictionless buying experience, businesses can capitalize on this trend and drive more sales through their social media channels.

Furthermore, the increasing emphasis on personalization and targeted content is a trend that cannot be ignored. As social media users become more discerning and demand more relevant and tailored experiences, businesses must invest in data-driven strategies to better understand their audience and deliver content that resonates with them on a deeper level. This might involve leveraging advanced analytics, machine learning, and customer segmentation to create hyper-personalized social media campaigns that cut through the noise and captivate their target consumers.

Another emerging trend in the social media landscape is the growing importance of community-building. As users seek deeper connections and a sense of belonging within their social networks, businesses that can cultivate thriving online communities around their brand will be poised for long-term success. This might involve fostering user-generated content, facilitating engaging discussions, and creating exclusive experiences or events that bring their loyal followers together.

Finally, the increasing emphasis on social media's role in driving real-world outcomes is a trend that savvy marketers should keep a close eye on. As the lines between digital and physical experiences continue to blur, businesses must find innovative ways to leverage social media to drive tangible, measurable results, whether that's in-store foot traffic, product sales, or brand awareness.

By staying ahead of these trends and adapting their social media marketing strategies accordingly, businesses can position themselves for success in the ever-evolving digital landscape. However, it's important to note that staying ahead of the curve in social media marketing is not a one-time event, but rather a continuous process of learning, experimentation, and adaptation.

Successful businesses will be those that are willing to embrace the uncertainty and flexibility required to navigate the constantly shifting social media landscape. By staying agile, innovative, and focused on the needs and behaviors of their target audience, they will be able to ride the waves of change and emerge as industry leaders in the years to come.

Case Studies of Successful Social Media Campaigns

Social media has revolutionized the way businesses and organizations connect with their audiences. Through carefully crafted campaigns, companies have been able to leverage the power of these platforms to drive brand awareness, increase engagement, and ultimately, achieve their marketing goals. In this chapter, we will explore several case studies that showcase successful social media campaigns, highlighting the strategies, tactics, and key takeaways that can be applied to diverse industries and business models.

Starbucks: RedCupContest

Starbucks, the global coffee giant, has long been known for its innovative approach to social media marketing. One of their most successful campaigns was the RedCupContest, which launched in 2014. The campaign was centered around the iconic red holiday cup that Starbucks introduces each year during the festive season.

The premise of the campaign was simple: customers were encouraged to share photos of themselves with the Starbucks red cup on social media, using the hashtag RedCupContest. The best submissions would be selected as winners, earning them various prizes, from free drinks to exclusive Starbucks merchandise.

The campaign was an instant hit, generating a significant amount of user-generated content (UGC) and driving engagement across social media platforms. Starbucks saw a surge in social media activity, with customers eagerly sharing their festive photos and competing for the coveted prizes.

The success of the RedCupContest can be attributed to several factors:

1. **Tapping into Seasonal Trends**: By aligning the campaign with the popular holiday season, Starbucks was able to capitalize on the heightened excitement and social media activity during this time of year.

2. **Leveraging User-Generated Content**: The contest encouraged customers to create and share their content, which not only generated a sense of community but also provided Starbucks with a wealth of user-generated visuals to utilize in their marketing efforts.

3. **Offering Attractive Prizes**: The prizes, ranging from free drinks to exclusive merchandise, provided a compelling incentive for customers to participate in the campaign, further driving engagement and social media activity.

The RedCupContest has become an annual tradition for Starbucks, with the campaign evolving and adapting to changing social media trends and customer preferences over the years. This case study demonstrates the power of leveraging seasonal themes, user-generated content, and attractive rewards to create a highly successful and engaging social media campaign.

Dove: RealBeauty

Dove, the personal care brand, has long been known for its emphasis on body positivity and self-esteem. In 2013, Dove launched its RealBeauty social media campaign, which aimed to challenge societal beauty standards and celebrate the diversity of women's bodies.

The campaign centered around a series of videos and images that featured "real" women of all shapes, sizes, and backgrounds, rather than the traditional idealized beauty standards often depicted in advertising. The campaign's message was clear: beauty comes in many forms, and Dove was committed to embracing and celebrating this diversity.

The RealBeauty campaign was a resounding success, generating significant engagement and positive sentiment across social media platforms. Customers responded enthusiastically to the campaign's message, sharing their own stories and experiences, and expressing their appreciation for Dove's inclusive approach.

The key factors that contributed to the success of the RealBeauty campaign include:

1. **Aligning with Brand Values**: The campaign was a natural extension of Dove's long-standing commitment to promoting body positivity and self-esteem, making it a seamless and authentic fit for the brand.

2. **Addressing a Societal Issue**: By tackling the prevalent issue of unrealistic beauty standards, Dove was able to tap into a broader cultural conversation and position itself as a champion for diversity and inclusion.

3. **Encouraging User Participation**: The campaign encouraged customers to share their own stories and experiences, fostering a sense of community and amplifying the campaign's message through user-generated content.

The RealBeauty campaign has continued to evolve and expand over the years, with Dove introducing new initiatives and content to further its mission of redefining beauty standards. This case study demonstrates the power of aligning a social media campaign with a brand's core values and addressing a relevant societal issue in a meaningful way.

Airbnb: Belong Anywhere

Airbnb, the global vacation rental platform, has long been known for its focus on creating a sense of belonging and community. In 2017, the company launched its Belong Anywhere social media campaign, which aimed to promote its mission of helping travelers feel at home wherever they go.

The campaign featured a series of emotive videos and images that showcased the diverse experiences and connections that Airbnb guests had made through their travels. The campaign's message was clear: Airbnb was not just about finding a place to stay, but about creating a sense of belonging and community in every destination.

The Belong Anywhere campaign was a resounding success, generating significant engagement and positive sentiment across social media platforms. Customers responded enthusiastically to the campaign's message, sharing their own stories and experiences of feeling at home with Airbnb and expressing their appreciation for the company's inclusive approach.

The key factors that contributed to the success of the Belong Anywhere campaign include:

1. **Aligning with Brand Values**: The campaign was a natural extension of Airbnb's mission of creating a sense of belonging and community, making it a seamless and authentic fit for the brand.

2. **Highlighting Emotional Connections**: By focusing on the emotional experiences and connections that Airbnb guests had made through their travels, the campaign was able to

tap into the universal human need for belonging and community.

3. **Encouraging User Participation**: The campaign encouraged customers to share their own stories and experiences, further amplifying the campaign's message and creating a sense of community among Airbnb users.

The Belong Anywhere campaign has continued to evolve and expand over the years, with Airbnb introducing new initiatives and content to further its mission of creating a more inclusive and welcoming travel experience. This case study demonstrates the power of aligning a social media campaign with a brand's core values and addressing a universal human need in a meaningful way.

The case studies presented in this chapter showcase the power of social media in driving brand awareness, engagement, and ultimately, marketing success. By leveraging seasonal trends, user-generated content, and emotional connections, these companies have been able to create highly effective and engaging social media campaigns that have resonated with their target audiences.

The key takeaways from these case studies include:

1. Aligning campaigns with brand values and addressing relevant societal issues

2. Encouraging user participation and leveraging user-generated content

3. Tapping into seasonal trends and cultural moments to capitalize on heightened social media activity

4. Highlighting emotional connections and universal human experiences

As businesses and organizations continue to navigate the ever-evolving landscape of social media, these case studies serve as inspiring examples of how to craft successful and impactful social media campaigns that can drive real results.

Conclusion

Building a strong, recognizable brand is essential for any business or individual looking to stand out in today's highly competitive marketplace. In the previous sections, we've explored the key components of a successful brand, from defining your unique value proposition to crafting a visually appealing and memorable brand identity.

However, in the digital age, simply having a great brand is not enough. To truly thrive, you need to focus on increasing your brand's reach and driving sales through the strategic use of social media platforms.

Social media has become the new frontier for connecting with your target audience and amplifying your brand's message. Platforms like Facebook, Instagram, Twitter, and LinkedIn offer businesses and individuals a cost-effective way to reach millions of potential customers, build meaningful relationships, and ultimately drive sales.

When used effectively, social media can be a powerful tool for expanding your brand's visibility, engaging with your audience, and generating a steady stream of new leads and sales. However, it's important to remember that social media marketing is not a one-size-fits-all approach. To truly maximize your results, you need to carefully tailor your strategy to the unique needs and preferences of your target audience.

One of the key ways to increase your brand's reach on social media is by creating and sharing high-quality, valuable content that resonates with your audience. This could include informative blog posts, eye-catching visuals, helpful tutorials, or engaging videos. By consistently providing your followers with content that is both entertaining and informative, you can build trust, establish your brand as an authority in your industry, and encourage users to share your content with their networks.

In addition to content creation, it's also important to focus on building a strong, engaged community on your social media platforms. This could involve actively responding to comments, running giveaways or contests, or hosting live Q&A sessions. By fostering a sense of community and connection, you can encourage users to not only follow your brand but also become loyal, engaged advocates.

Another crucial aspect of social media marketing is leveraging the power of influencers and thought leaders within your industry. By partnering with individuals who have a large, engaged following, you can tap into new audiences and leverage their credibility to boost your brand's visibility and trustworthiness.
Whether it's through sponsored posts, product collaborations, or guest appearances, working with the right influencers can be a highly effective way to drive sales and increase your brand's reach.

Of course, to truly maximize the impact of your social media efforts, it's important to carefully track and analyze your performance. By monitoring metrics like engagement rates, click-through rates, and conversion rates, you can continuously refine your strategy and identify the most effective tactics for reaching your target audience and driving sales.

Building a strong, recognizable brand is essential for any business or individual looking to succeed in today's highly competitive marketplace. By leveraging the power of social media to increase your brand's reach and drive sales, you can unlock a world of new opportunities and position your brand for long-term success.

Building a successful brand is not a one-time event, but an ongoing process that requires dedication, creativity, and a deep understanding of your target audience. By consistently delivering value, fostering a sense of community, and adapting your strategy to the ever-changing social media landscape, you can position your brand as a trusted, industry-leading voice that resonates with your audience and drives real, measurable results.

www.ingramcontent.com/pod-product-compliance
Lightning Source LLC
Chambersburg PA
CBHW050114230526
45470CB00004B/1830